Annaleise Carr

*How I conquered Lake Ontario
to help kids battling cancer*

Annaleise Carr
as told to Deborah Ellis

James Lorimer & Company Ltd., Publishers
Toronto

James Lorimer & Company Ltd., Publishers acknowledges the support of the Ontario Arts Council. We acknowledge the financial support of the Government of Canada through the Canada Book Fund for our publishing activities. We acknowledge the support of the Canada Council for the Arts which last year invested $24.3 million in writing and publishing throughout Canada. We acknowledge the Government of Ontario through the Ontario Media Development Corporation's Ontario Book Initiative.

Cover design: Meredith Bangay
Cover image: Dr. Mark Ghesquiere

Library and Archives Canada Cataloguing in Publication

Carr, Annaleise, 1998, author
    Annaleise Carr : how I conquered Lake Ontario to help kids battling cancer / Annaleise Carr ; as told to Deborah Ellis.

(Record books)
Includes index.
Issued in print and electronic formats.
ISBN 978-1-4594-0631-5 (pbk.).--ISBN 978-1-4594-0632-2 (bound).--ISBN 978-1-4594-0633-9 (epub)

    1. Carr, Annaleise, 1998-. 2. Swimmers--Canada--Biography--Juvenile literature. 3. Women swimmers--Canada--Biography--Juvenile literature. 4. Long distance swimming--Ontario, Lake (N.Y. and Ont.)--Juvenile literature. I. Ellis, Deborah, 1960-, author II. Title. III. Series: Record books

GV838.C37A3 2014   j797.2'1092   C2013-908158-5
                                           C2013-908159-3

James Lorimer & Company Ltd., Publishers
317 Adelaide Street West, Suite 1002
Toronto, ON, Canada
M5V 1P9
www.lorimer.ca

Distributed in the United States by:
Orca Book Publishers
P.O. Box 468
Custer, WA USA
98240-0468

Printed and bound in Canada.
Manufactured by Friesens Corporation in Altona, Manitoba, Canada in August 2014.
Job #205581

*To Camp Trillium,
and kids with cancer,
and to all those who
helped me across
"the Lake."*

Contents

Foreword

by the Hon. David C. Onley, O.Ont.
Lieutenant Governor of Ontario

One day a spirited girl named Annaleise Carr swam across Lake Ontario and straight into our hearts. This book tells her inspiring story — how a fourteen-year-old braved the high waves to help children with cancer.

As Annaleise knows, kids with cancer face challenges as big as her own. They, too, are on a journey. And like her, they face physical and mental hardships. Some are even fighting for their lives.

When Annaleise first visited Camp Trillium, she met these brave kids. She saw how much the camp cheered them. Right away, she wanted to help. Too young to volunteer at the camp, she decided to help in her own special way.

Annaleise has a rare gift. She can swim very well and very far. This gift of hers has grown stronger, the more she has used it. After ten years of swimming in competitions — since the age of four! — Annaleise was ready to tackle the biggest challenge of her young life.

She set a very exciting goal: she would swim right across Lake Ontario to raise funds for Camp Trillium. Encouraged by her sister and her parents, Annaleise began to plan her "radical crossing" with a loyal team of supporters.

After much training, she was ready for the big day.

You can read all about her daring

adventure in this book — how she kept herself going for nearly 27 hours, swimming through the rough waves, all the way from Niagara-on-the-Lake to Marilyn Bell Park in Toronto.

You can also learn about the kids at Camp Trillium who inspired her crossing. Annaleise has touched their lives in a very special way. And her remarkable story has touched us, too.

I have met Annaleise several times and am always impressed by her brave spirit. I have presented her with both the Lieutenant Governor's Community Volunteer Award and the Ontario Junior Citizens of the Year Award. The prime minister has given her the Queen Elizabeth II Diamond Jubilee Medal.

These are just a few of the tributes that have come her way.

Clearly, Annaleise Carr is a wonderful role model for young people. As the youngest person ever to swim across Lake Ontario, she has shown rare courage and endurance. And best of all, her achievement has helped other kids to face their own challenges with courage and endurance, too.

Since her crossing, Annaleise has been invited to tell her story to many people. And now she has created this book to share her message with you. Read on and see the great good that comes when we share our best gifts with others.

May these stories inspire you!

Hon. David C. Onley

Prologue

My name is Annaleise Rebekah Carr. I am 15 years old and in my second year of high school.

On August 18, 2012, when I was 14, I became the youngest person so far to swim across Lake Ontario.

Swimming has been a big part of my life for almost my whole life. I started swimming in competitions before I started kindergarten. I was fast and I could keep going for a long time.

When I was a little kid, my coach would put me into races with 18-year-olds, just casual races, to see how I would do. The big boys would say things like "Oh, we'll have to let the little kid win," but they never did. That wouldn't be much of a victory, anyway, if someone lets you win! But I did pretty well against them.

My grandmother likes to tell this story of when she took me to a swim meet in Woodstock when I was five. She says someone came up to me afterwards and asked for my autograph, because they said I was going to do great things! She may have been exaggerating — after all, she's my grandmother!

I'm really short and I don't have much of a reach with my arms, so I have a disadvantage when it comes to racing sprints. Many champion sprint swimmers are very tall. Taller, longer swimmers have an easier time getting ahead faster.

In the longer races, though, I have an advantage — and that advantage is that I never give up!

Lake Ontario is the smallest of the five Great Lakes, but it is still plenty big! It is the 14th-largest lake in the world. Currents flowing into it from Niagara Falls make it one of the toughest open-water swims to complete.

I would not be the first person to do it. The first one to complete the swim was Marilyn Bell, finishing on September 9, 1954. It earned her the nickname "Lady of the Lake." A few dozen other swimmers have made the crossing since then. Many others have tried and have been pulled out of the water — the waves, the current, and the cold temperature of the lake tired them out, and they were not able to complete their swim.

I did not know when I decided to do the swim what level of work the swim would require — from me, from my family, and from my supporters. I did not know then how hard it would be.

Maybe that's best when we start on an unknown journey. We can prepare as much as possible beforehand, but when we finally start out, that first step is really a leap of faith.

There are a few things people might want to know about me.

I love my family — my mother Debbie, my father Jeff, my sisters Larissa and McKenna, my brother Ayden, and all my grandparents, cousins, aunts, and uncles. My faith and my family give me strength.

I love living in Norfolk County, which is in Southern Ontario. My grandfather is a farmer here, and we still live in the old family farmhouse.

I love Canada, deep-fried Mars bars, cheerleading, triathlons and riding my bike.

I hate seeing children hurt.

And that is why I decided to swim across the lake.

Looking out over the water — like a second home! Dr. Mark Ghesquiere.

1 Special Kids

This whole journey began with my first visit to Camp Trillium.

My swim team for pool swimming is the Norfolk Hammerheads. The team I swim with for open-water swimming is called the North Shore Runners and Swimmers, out of Port Dover, on Lake Erie.

Every year, my open-water swim team puts together a 10-K Lake Erie swim for the fun and challenge of doing it, and to

At the rainbow gates of Camp Trillium. Jeff Carr.

raise money for a good cause. For several years, the club raised money for the fight against breast cancer.

Since there are a lot of events around breast cancer, one of my teammates suggested we do something different. Camp Trillium came up as a possibility.

We didn't know much about it, except that it's in Norfolk County and is for children with cancer. We decided to pay them a visit to learn more.

We drove up together, got out of the van and started the tour.

I saw a little kid with no hair.

She was lagging a bit behind the others in the group, but not for long. The other kids stopped, looked back at her and retraced their steps so that she could run with them.

No one complained about it or nagged at her to hurry up.

I didn't hear any unkind words.

All I heard was laughter.

"People hear the word 'cancer' and they automatically think it's a death sentence," the camp director, our tour guide, said. "That may have been true a few years ago, and it is still true in too many parts of the world. But here in Canada, 78 per cent of children diagnosed with cancer will still be living five years after their diagnosis, and 70 per cent of those children will become long-term survivors of cancer."

What is cancer?

Every living thing is made up of millions of cells. These cells regularly divide to make new cells and the old cells die off. If a cell becomes damaged, it can mutate. When the mutated cell divides, the mutation continues to grow. Cancer comes from the damage caused by these abnormal cells.

Cancer can affect any part of the body. There are more than a hundred types of cancer. The most common types of cancer children get are brain and nervous system cancers, cancers of the kidneys, bones, muscles and lymphatic system, and leukemia.

In the 1950s, less than 10 per cent of cancer in children could be cured. Now, the cure rate is 75 per cent, which climbs to 90 per cent for leukemia.

It must be scary, though, I thought.

I looked at all the kids, playing, talking, and hanging out.

They didn't look scared to me.

They just looked like . . . kids!

A place to play at Camp Trillium. Jeff Carr.

"One of the side effects of cancer treatment is hair loss," the director said. "The chemotherapy has to be strong to kill the cancer cells. Unfortunately that means it is strong enough to kill the healthy cells, too."

She went on to say that not everyone reacts to chemo in the same way, and that kids come to the camp in all different stages of their cancer journey.

"We also take the brothers and sisters of the child with cancer," she said. "Cancer might be diagnosed in just one person, but that diagnosis affects the whole family."

I kept looking at the kids, sure that I could pick out which kids were sick and which kids were healthy. But I couldn't tell.

"Generally, you won't notice the difference between the kids with cancer and the kids who don't have cancer," the director said, as if she was reading my mind. "Everyone is treated the same. Except for whatever medical needs the child has. We have nurses on-site who specialize in childhood cancer."

The director showed us the main hall where the kitchen was, and where the people ate their meals and held gatherings during bad weather. She showed us the neat wooden cabins, the playground, firepit and beach.

"Our lake is called Rainbow Lake," she

Go look at a tree

Scientific studies have shown that spending time in nature is good for our health. Being around trees, grass, and flowers — any outdoor, natural setting — can lower blood pressure, make it easier to get to sleep, cheer us up, lower stress and make our bodies better able to fight infections.

said. "It's a private lake, just for us. One of the challenges we try to do with each camp session is to get kids to swim across the lake."

I looked out across Rainbow Lake. It was not a big lake, by any means, but to a little kid who isn't used to swimming, it must seem enormous.

Again the camp director read my mind.

"They go out in a group," she said. "All swimmers — adults, kids, strong swimmers, new swimmers — have to wear life jackets. There are boats that go with them, in case they need to get out of the water and take a rest. You can imagine how powerful they feel when they make it across the lake."

"It's a metaphor," I said, remembering my seventh-grade English classes. "The battle with the lake is like their battle with cancer."

"That's exactly right," the director said. "Sometimes the cancer battle does not let the child have a lot of victories. One stage in the battle ends, then another one begins. Swimming across Rainbow Lake is not impossible for them, but it is just hard enough for them to know how brave and strong they are."

Standing on the shore, it was easy for me to imagine the courage it would take, and the blind faith, for a little kid, weak from cancer and the cancer treatment, to step into the lake and start swimming.

It would be harder for that kid than for

a healthy person to swim across one of the Great Lakes.

"I'd like to volunteer here," I said suddenly. I may have interrupted the camp director, I was so excited. "I'd love to come here and help out. I'm very responsible — you can ask anyone."

The camp director smiled. It was a kind smile, but I could tell she didn't take me seriously.

She probably gets kids all the time saying they want to volunteer, and then the kids forget about it, I thought. *She doesn't know me. When I get an idea in my head, I don't back down.*

"How old are you?" the camp director asked.

"Thirteen," I said.

"Give me a call in five years," she said. "We don't take any volunteers before they are eighteen. Right now, you are too young."

Too young? I didn't like the thought of having to wait for five years.

The camp director went on to talk about archery and crafts and the youth programs and leadership training, but I was really only half-listening. My mind was focused on my disappointment. I really wanted to help in some way.

I thought about it during the rest of the tour.

By the time I got back in the van to go home, I had an idea.

2  Getting Ready

The first person I told my idea to was my sister Larissa.

I am the oldest child in my family. Larissa is next to me in age, followed by my sister McKenna and my brother Ayden. I needed Larissa's advice on how to tell my parents.

"You want to swim across the whole lake?" she asked.

"No," I replied, tossing a pillow at her. All three of us sisters share a bedroom.

"I'll just swim halfway across, then I'll turn around and come back. Yes, the whole lake! Just like Marilyn Bell did."

"Can you do that?" Larissa asked. "I mean, I know people have done it — but do you really think *you* can do it?"

"I think I can, if I train for it," I said. "What do you think Mom and Dad will say?"

"They'll say no," Larissa said. "They'll say you're too young, it's too dangerous

Larissa, McKenna, Ayden, and I. Jeff Carr.

and it will interfere with school. Then, after they say all that and you tell them you still want to do it, they'll say yes."

I laughed, because that was exactly how I thought it would go, too. Once I have an idea to do something, I don't want to *not* do it.

I brought up my idea to my parents over supper, and it went just like Larissa and I thought it would.

First, they laughed. Then, when they realized I was serious, they got scared. They know how determined I can be, and they did not want me doing something dangerous.

I had done some research beforehand.

"I won't be out there all by myself," I said. "Marilyn Bell had a coach who went with her in a boat, keeping an eye on her and feeding her. Others have done it, too. If they can do it, maybe I can do it, too."

About Lake Ontario

Lake Ontario is 311 km long, 83 km across at its widest point, and as much as 244 metres deep. It is the smallest of the 5 Great Lakes, and the 14th-largest freshwater lake in the world.

Where the Niagara River enters Lake Ontario, it sends a current rushing to the bottom of the lake. This current crosses the lake, rising again near Toronto and bringing up cold water from the bottom.

We kept talking about it, and finally they said yes, we could look into it.

"How much do you think I could raise for Camp Trillium?" I asked them. "Do you think it could be as much as $30,000?"

They thought maybe the swim could raise that much, but I could tell they were not really committed to the idea yet. Neither was my Aunt Lisa, who came over that night and learned about my plan.

My Aunt Lisa is funny and wonderful, but although she said all the right things when I told her, I could tell she did not really believe I could do it.

That was okay. At least I had their go-ahead to start planning.

Then the work really began.

I wanted to do the swim the next summer, which would give me eight months to train. I knew about training. It was just a matter of making a commitment and sticking to it. If I just decided that this is what I wanted to do, then the decision was made. I didn't have to think each day about whether or not to train that day. I just had to do the workouts.

So I knew I would train, but I didn't know *how* I had to train for a lake crossing. I needed to get a coach.

One of the coaches with the Norfolk Hammerheads was Lisa Anderson. I asked her to be my coach for this crossing, and

Enjoying the sun and the water. Cindy Pichette, Silver Parrot Studio.

was thrilled when she agreed.

I would need boats, too, and food, and I'd need to collect sponsorships to cover the cost of the swim, as well as raise money for Camp Trillium, and . . . everything I thought of to do led to many other things to do. I started to make a list. The list got longer after I learned about Solo Swims of Ontario.

Back in the 1970s, a man died while he was trying to swim across Lake Ontario. After that happened, there was a government inquiry. Solo Swims of Ontario came out of that inquiry. Its purpose is to set safety guidelines and rules about who can attempt to swim across one of the Great Lakes or Georgian Bay.

I liked what they had to say: "For every marathon swimmer, the challenge is to beat the lake, complete the swim, to go all the way and, to meet this challenge, a marathon swimmer must have good planning, determination, dedication, strength, endurance, and good luck. The swimmer must be mentally and physically prepared, well trained and committed."

Their information goes on to say: "Anyone considering the challenge of a long distance solo swim in Ontario must have the swim sanctioned by Solo Swims of Ontario, Inc."

When I saw the rule book, I could tell they were serious. The book has almost 70 pages! I would have to get medical clearance, get permits from the Toronto Harbour Master and, if I wanted to touch land at Marilyn Bell Park, I would need to check first to make sure some other swimmer hadn't booked it ahead of me. As well, there was a rather expensive registration fee — $1000.

All of this told me two important things.

One was that, while I was going to be in the water alone, I would be making the journey with many other people who would be there in spirit, or floating in boats beside me.

The race to be the first

When Marilyn Bell completed her swim in 1954, she was racing against two other swimmers for prize money and as part of the entertainment for that year's Canadian National Exhibition. Florence Chadwick, an American, was already a famous long-distance swimmer, and people expected her to win. The other swimmer, Winnie Roach Leuszler, had already swum across the English Channel. Sixteen-year-old Marilyn had the least experience of all three.

There were high waves that night. They made Florence Chadwick too sick to continue. Winnie got horrible cramps and was pulled from the water with only a quarter of the journey still to go.

The second was that I would need lots of help to get everything in place.

When I tackle my homework, I like to do one subject at a time, focusing on it and getting it done. It was a system that had worked well for me — I maintained an above-80 average.

I would need to apply the same focus for the next eight months in order make this swim happen.

Bit by bit, it all started to come together. One bit of luck was that I would be old enough — but just by a few months. The minimum age for a lake crossing is 14. I would turn 14 in March and planned to do the swim in August.

"Your swim needs a name," my father said. "Something to get people interested. 'Swim for Camp Trillium' or 'Swimming for the Kids'? Any ideas?"

"What about something with your initials?" Larissa suggested. "Annaleise Rebekah Carr — A.R.C. Annaleise's Radical Crossing."

I liked the sound of that.

Over the next few months, forms were filled out, permits were gotten, a crew was recruited and posters were put up all over Norfolk County. I would walk through the town of Simcoe, see my posters in the shop windows and think, *Wow, I'm actually doing this!*

Some days, it was a little hard for even me to believe.

3 So Many New Friends

Lots of people came on-board. They admired the work of Camp Trillium and they wanted to do something to help. I was amazed at the way an idea could, bit by bit, become a reality.

We got a website up explaining what the Radical Crossing was all about. It promoted the fundraising events we were doing.

There were so many things that had to be done — and I still had to finish the eighth grade! Without my parents and people in the community working on this swim, it never would have happened. Often when people helped out, they would say, "My mother died of cancer," or "I lost my friend to cancer." I think that helping the kids at Camp Trillium was a way for them to honour the person they lost.

There were lots of events and fundraisers leading up to the swim. We had wristbands made and we sold them. We had a table at Toronto City Hall on a community awareness day that the city had. We did a fundraiser at Long Point Eco Adventures and another at The Barrel restaurant in Simcoe. At Eisings Greenhouses, all the money from one type of plant sold on one day went to the swim. People bought lots of plants and even made donations. At the Friendship Festival, Simcoe's annual event over the Civic Holiday long weekend,

I was Grand Marshal of the parade and raised some money, too.

The local news media in Norfolk County helped spread the word. I did interviews with the radio station CD98.9 and with newspapers like the *Hub* and the *Simcoe Reformer*.

When Marilyn Bell did her swim across the lake, the *Toronto Star* sent along a reporter in one of her boats to write about the event as it happened. When it started to look like my plans for a crossing were more than just a kid dreaming about some unattainable future, the *Toronto Star* decided to send a reporter and a boat out onto the lake with me, too.

One of the great sponsors we got was the RE7 sports drink. This drink was new and wasn't even available for sale yet in Canada. It's a healthy sports drink, not too sweet, and tastes sort of like a melted blue slushie. The guy who invented it heard about my swim and flew in from Calgary to meet me and my family. He asked if I needed a sports drink, then gave me a lifetime supply!

The folks at Camp Trillium put information about the crossing in their newsletter, the one they send out to all the families who go to their camps. That newsletter led us to the Thomas family. The dad, Alistair, called us one night.

"Our son had cancer, and both of our kids have spent time at Camp Trillium," Alistair said. "We are all excited about your swim. Assisting you is a way for our family to give back for all we received from Camp Trillium. We live in Mississauga. How can we help? Do you have anyone to organize things for you in Toronto?"

My family met the Thomas family and liked them right away.

They have two sons. Their oldest son, Eric, is the one who was diagnosed with

The wonderful Thomas family. Jeff Carr.

cancer. Their youngest son's name is Aiden — the same name as my brother's, but with a different spelling! Just as my decision to swim across Lake Ontario affected the whole family, Eric's cancer diagnosis affected the whole family, too. We had a lot in common.

So many people were getting excited about my swim and were stepping forward to be part of it. There were times, late at night, I would have trouble falling asleep, because I worried that I might let all these people down.

I trained hard, doing at least six workouts in the pool every week.

One of the ways Coach Lisa had me train was on a tether. She would tie me to a starting block with an elastic chord and make me swim in place for hours.

"This will build up your strength and give you the experience of swimming really hard without moving very far. You never know what kind of conditions you will meet out on the lake! This will train your mind, too, so that it can deal with the monotony of the hours of swimming."

I had dry-land training, too — running to strengthen my legs, and weights to strengthen my core. In May we started training in the lake. Sometimes I trained in Lake Erie. Sometimes I trained with the Lake Ontario Swimmers Team (LOST) in Oakville. It meant a lot of very early mornings and a lot of driving for my parents. August was coming up fast.

Glycogen

When we eat carbohydrates, they break down into sugars that are used for energy. Any sugar not needed right away gets stored in muscles and in the liver as glycogen. Once the body has used as much glycogen as it can, the rest of the sugar is turned into fat.

Athletes burn glycogen when they exercise, especially short, intense exercise. In longer, slower exercise, athletes draw on their stores of fat for energy, with glycogen helping to turn that fat into fuel.

Quick sources of energy, or simple carbohydrates, are things like fruit, pastries and candy. Complex carbohydrates are absorbed more slowly and generally provide more nutrients. Whole-grain breads, pasta, rice, beans and vegetables are examples of complex carbohydrates.

Solo Swims of Ontario requires every Lake Ontario crosser to do a qualifying swim of 16 kilometres so that they know the person is able to swim a long way.

I did the 18 kilometres in six hours and swam over a big school of fish.

"You are ready for this physically," Coach Lisa told me, "but you already know that this is mostly a mental challenge. Your head will keep you going even if your body is tired, but if your head tells you to stop, it doesn't matter how much energy and strength you have left in your body — you will be able to convince yourself to stop. So, I have an idea."

She wanted me to make a movie.

"Two movies, actually," she said. "Make them up in your head and run them over and over so that you can see all the details. Then, when you are swimming, you can call up these movies and they will help you keep your head where it needs to be."

One of the "movies" we came up with was of me touching the wall at Marilyn Bell Park in Toronto. This is the place that Marilyn touched when she finished

The rock at Queen's Royal Park with the names of everyone who has made the swim across Lake Ontario. Jeff Carr.

her historic swim. I knew what that spot looked like.

There is a rock in Queen's Royal Park in Niagara-on-the-Lake. Everyone who completes the Lake Ontario swim gets their name carved in that rock. I wanted my name there, too. So I added that scene to the movie in my head.

The other movie I made up was about

The office at Camp Trillium. Jeff Carr.

going through the gates at Camp Trillium and presenting the director with a cheque for the money I raised on the swim. I knew what the camp looked like. I knew the staff and I knew the beauty and fun of the place. That was an easy movie to make up.

Finally, the time came to leave my home in Walsh and head to Niagara-on-the-Lake. I double-checked that I had everything I needed and got in the van with my family.

Pulling away from the house was sort of surreal. I would be a different person the next time I walked through my front door. If I was able to complete the crossing, I would be different because I had met a very difficult challenge. If I was unable to complete the crossing — if the weather got bad, or if I wasn't properly prepared, or if I just lost my nerve — then I would be another sort of person.

While I knew there was no shame in being beaten back by weather or by stomach cramps — better swimmers than I had been pulled out of the water, some right within sight of the shore — I didn't want to know how that would feel, coming home without achieving my goal.

I had to make it to the other side.

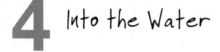4 Into the Water

It looked like an awfully big lake.

I stood in Queen's Royal Park in Niagara-on-the-Lake, at the edge of Lake Ontario, looking out across the lake. Behind me was a huge crowd of people, all cheering. It was August 18, 2012, just after six o'clock in the evening. The swim had already been delayed a day because of the weather. We stayed in the White Oaks Resort in Niagara, a great place, but I wanted to get going!

The delay in the start meant that there was time for more media interviews. Media people had contacted me at home in Walsh before we left, and I even filmed something for *The National,* the CBC TV news program that goes all across the country. Another TV interview I filmed was played over and over again on a news program that was on the television sets in the elevators at White Oaks — every time we walked into the elevator, there I was, talking about the swim!

People were so nice. We were having dinner in the restaurant at the hotel, and when the news clip came on TV, the staff brought us free truffles!

Finally, we were almost ready for the swim to start.

I stood on the edge of the lake, looking across all that water. I could see the Toronto skyline. It looked very far away.

I wondered if Marilyn Bell, the Lady of

the Lake, was this scared before she started her swim.

If she can do it, I can do it, I told myself.

But she was 16, I remembered. I was only 14.

All those voices came back to me, the voices of people saying, "You're too small! The lake is too big!"

Were they right?

Then I heard another voice.

"There must be five hundred people here," my mother said. She was standing close by with the rest of my family.

"More like a thousand," my father said.

"You're already famous and you haven't even done anything yet!"

This came from my sister Larissa. My whole family was there to see me off, even my grandparents.

"You know that, whether you finish the swim or not, we think you are a winner just for caring enough to try."

That had been my family's message all along. They believed I could finish the swim, but they wanted me to know it would be okay with them if I couldn't.

More voices started to reach me.

"Annaleise! Annaleise! You can do it!"

I knew that the crowd behind me was full of supporters. Many were people I didn't know, and some were friends I didn't expect to see.

There were many people from the press there, too.

"You are a story for them," Coach Lisa had told me before we came down to the water. "You will be the youngest person ever to swim across Lake Ontario. The press will want to talk to you as you walk from the car to the shore. They will ask you all kinds of questions and want you to comment. My advice is to not talk to them then. There will be opportunities later. Right now you will need to focus on the swim."

It was good advice. I was worried that they would think I was rude, but Coach Lisa said the press would understand.

I was glad the press was so interested. When they talked and wrote about my swim, they would also have to talk about *why* I was swimming. More people would learn about Camp Trillium and the terrific families who go there. I was too young to be one of their volunteers, but not too young to swim across the lake for them!

I stood back from the water. It was too soon to go in. All the support boats and the crew needed to get into place.

My skin was greased up with lanolin to protect it from being cut where the straps of my bathing suit rubbed it. Wetsuits are not allowed for official lake crossings under the rules set by Solo Swims of Ontario. I had to wear my ordinary bathing suit. I was fine with that. It was what I was used to. There would be enough new things happening on this journey across the lake.

The lanolin would also help protect me from the cold. Lake Ontario is the second-deepest of the five Great Lakes. Surface temperatures, even in the summer, can go down to ten degrees Celsius.

Hypothermia has been a problem for other swimmers. I didn't want to get so cold that I couldn't complete the swim.

My shoulders were slathered with zinc oxide, a sunscreen. Without it, I could get badly sunburned. The sun would bounce off the water and be very intense.

I gave my arms and legs a shake. The boats were nearly in place. The Humber College sailing crew had sailed their sailboats across from Toronto the day before. The White Oaks Resort had given us a really great deal, since so many of the crew had to stay over.

"Ready?" Mom asked.

I nodded.

She and Dad didn't try to talk me out of

Hypothermia

Core body temperature for most people is 37 Celsius, or 98.6 Fahrenheit. Hypothermia is a condition that happens when exposure to severe or prolonged cold makes the body's heat drop faster than it can be revved up again. If the core temperature drops even just a few degrees, hypothermia sets in. Cold water makes the body lose heat faster than cold air does.

Shivering is the body's way of trying to create enough energy to warm itself up. In its severest form, hypothermia can lead to the body shutting down and even to death. Signs of hypothermia include:

• shivering that won't stop
• slower breathing
• slower heart rate
• paler skin
• blue look to hands, ears or lips
• confusion

The treatment for hypothermia in swimmers is simple. The swimmer gets out of the water, removes wet clothing, wraps up in dry blankets and drinks something hot. In severe cases, the swimmer needs medical care.

it. All those conversations had happened already, over the months of training to prepare for the crossing. I knew they were proud of me whether or not I did the swim. I also knew that, while they had a lot of faith in my ability as an athlete, they were also a little bit afraid. A lot could happen in the middle of such a big lake. But now, at this final moment, they kept their fear to themselves.

"See you on the other side," Dad said.

Then they stepped back to give me one last minute to prepare myself for what lay ahead.

"Don't be afraid," I heard my grandmother say. "Look at your hand."

On my hand I had written "Ephesians 3:14-21" in waterproof ink.

It was a Bible verse, from Paul's letter to the Ephesians. It means that God's love and protection is stronger than the wind and bigger than the depths of the lake.

"It will remind you that you're not

Swimming gear

Swimming caps made from spandex, neoprene or latex, do not keep a swimmer's hair dry, but they do keep hair out of a swimmer's face. They also help to keep a swimmer warm. Open-water swimmers tend to choose bright colours so they can be seen easily in the water.

Earplugs can provide swimmers who have had ear infections with extra protection, although they also make it harder for the swimmer to hear.

The first swimming goggles were designed in the 1970s. Before that, swimmers who wanted eye protection had to wear large, awkward snorkel masks.

Some **goggles** come with special seals to prevent leaks. Goggles can come with tinted lenses to reduce the glare of the sun off the water. They can also come with prescription lenses for those who need glasses to see properly.

alone out there," Mom said.

The beginning of the passage reads: "Then we shall no longer be children, carried by the waves, and blown about by every shifting wind . . ."

It is about being watched over and taken care of — something it would be good to remember when I was out in the middle of the lake.

Finally I got the signal.

They were ready for me to step into the water.

I can't do this, I thought.

And then I remembered the kids at Camp Trillium.

They were dealing with cancer. Every morning they and their families got up and faced another day of treatment, of doctor visits, of medical tests, of pain, of fear and of hope. But when they got to camp, they laughed and played and sang goofy camp songs as if life were fine, as if they were

Greased up and ready to dive in and start swimming. Jared Krause.

just regular kids at a regular camp.

They were the brave ones, I thought. All I had to do was swim.

I knew how to do that.

I looked again at the Bible verse on my hand.

I wouldn't be in the water alone.

It's time, I said to myself.

I took one last look at my sister Larissa.

Then I took a step forward and went into the lake.

5 Swimming with the Sunset

"You're making great time!" Coach Lisa shouted. "In fact, you're on track to set a new time record if you can keep this up!"

The lake was flat, with barely a ripple disturbing the surface. I was feeling really good. I used the front crawl swimming stroke, the one I had trained with. My arms and legs were working just as they were supposed to. I was breathing in a good rhythm, just like I did during all my training swims. Take three strokes, breathe

Breathing

While doing the crawl, some swimmers prefer to take a breath by turning their head to only one side. But open-water swimmers cannot count on calm conditions. They need to be equally comfortable taking a breath from both left and right.

to the left, take three strokes, then breathe to the right. I knew I was surrounded by great people because I could see them every time I took a breath.

When I breathed to the left, I could see Rob Smith, the guy in the kayak. His job was to keep an eye on me. If I ran into trouble, he could probably get to me faster than the folks in the boats. Each time I looked in his direction, I could see him smiling at me.

When I took a breath to the right, I could see my Aunt Lisa on the boat. She was in charge of the food for the crew

Making good time at the beginning of the swim. Dr. Mark Ghesquiere.

on the trip. She's a great cook and an even greater kidder. It's impossible to feel uncomfortable around her — even when she's trying to embarrass us!

In the Zodiac with my coach was John Bulsza, the swim master with Solo Swims of Ontario. He was along to make sure that all the rules were followed, kind of an official witness to my breaking the record. He had done other crossings with other swimmers. He knew the lake really well — the currents, the weather, old shipwrecks and superstitions. And he told really bad jokes.

Dr. Mark Ghesquiere was on the boat, too. Before I went into the water he had me swallow a capsule that would monitor my core temperature through the entire swim. He could keep an eye on my temperature through a monitor. This would help him to know if I was getting hypothermia, which can be very dangerous.

There was one kayak, two sailboats, two Zodiacs and one other boat — six boats around me, all filled with people watching out for me.

I can do this, I thought as my arms pulled me through the water. I had trained hard. I knew how to swim and I had good people around me — I could really do this! Sixteen hours — that's how long

Support boats

Kayaks are narrow, low boats that usually hold only one or two people. The top of the boat is covered or closed except for a hole where the paddler sits. The closed top provides protection from the cold waters and bad weather. The paddler pushes the kayak through the water with a single pole that has a paddle on each end.

Humans have been using them for thousands of years. They originated in the Arctic, northern British Columbia and the Siberian coast.

A **Zodiac** is an inflatable rubber watercraft with a motor. Their speed and agility makes them a perfect choice for life-saving and rescue work.

they thought it would take me to cross the lake. Fifty-two kilometres in 16 hours. I started around six in the evening, so I should be finished around ten o'clock the next morning.

Sixteen hours is a long time, but I decided not to think about that. I decided I would only think about being in the water, taking the next stroke and reaching the other side.

The water was smooth, the wind was quiet, and everything was going great.

I could hear the cheering crowds for quite a while after I started swimming. Now, though, it was just quiet.

There is something really special about being able to swim. I imagine it is sort of what it would feel like to be able to fly. Human beings are supposed to live on land. We were not really made to be in the water. We have no fins or feathers, our feet and hands are not webbed, we have lungs that can only hold so much air, and our bodies have very little natural protection from the cold. It really is something that we figured out — that being in the water is a good thing, that we can move ourselves through it and feel comfortable in it.

As the gang on the boats laughed and played music, I started to wonder about the first people to go in the water. What made them go in? I learned in school about ancient civilizations in the Middle East and in central Africa. Were they out fishing and their boat tipped over, and they realized that if they moved their arms and kicked their legs, they could stay afloat? And did they tell their friends back on shore, maybe taught them what they learned? If people are not afraid, is it as natural for them to swim as it is to walk?

There were lots of things to think about, and I had 16 hours to think about them. Maybe just 15 hours now. But I did not want to ask how much time had passed. I didn't think it would be good for me to know. I decided to just swim and let time take care of itself.

I do a lot of running to get ready for swimming, because running is so good for the leg muscles. Swimming a long way is like running a long way. You get into a rhythm. You send your brain into a space where it can roam freely, and let your body just do the work.

Take three strokes, breathe to the left. Take three more strokes, breathe to the right. Repeat. And repeat. And repeat.

I swam, and I listened to the crew laugh and talk, and I felt very good and very relaxed.

"You should eat something now," Coach Lisa said after a bit.

We had spent a lot of time practicing the feeding and eating ritual in the weeks before the race. We used a lacrosse stick, with the food or drink in the basket end of it.

Solo Swims of Ontario rules say that if I accidentally touched the basket while getting the food out of it, I would not be disqualified. But I was not allowed to grab hold of it. Often by the time I got hold of the food, it was wet from the waves. I learned to eat it anyway.

Coach Lisa passed me a Jell-O shot mixed with cottage cheese and yogurt. When I got that down, she passed me some RE7 to drink.

Refreshed, I started swimming again.

A while later, I noticed that the light was changing. The lake looked silvery and the air was getting cooler. The sun was starting to go down.

The sky was incredible. It was a mixture of colours — reds and oranges and yellows and purples. I thought I had the best viewpoint, being right at eye level with the water and the horizon. I watched the sun as it appeared to drop into the lake. The purples started to take over the sky.

"That was really special," I heard someone say.

They were right. It *was* special.

It was also the last time I would see the sun for ten hours.

The hardest part was coming next. Darkness. I had never really swum in the darkness before. I hoped I would be able to do it.

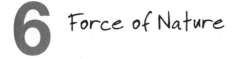

6 Force of Nature

As the sun went down, the waves came up.

I like waves and generally really enjoy swimming in them. There is a rush that comes with a wave, and when I push through it, it feels like a contest between the wave and me.

But there was a big difference between swimming in waves for fun — with the option to get out of the water close at hand — and the waves that were coming at me that night.

I was also not used to swimming in darkness. I had done one short night swim before this. That swim was to test the light strapped onto my bathing cap, to see if it could be seen from the boat and to check other things, like the radio and the spacing for the support boats.

I knew I was surrounded by boats and by people who would spend the night looking out for me. I couldn't always see them, but I knew they were there. It was like the Bible verse on my hand. I could not always see God, but I knew that God was there and I was protected.

Knowing all that, though, did not mean I didn't get scared. The waves were getting bigger, and the night had just started.

Solo Swim Ontario's rules state that for the first five hours of a swim, no one can be in the water with the swimmer. Later on, they allow pacers to get in. A pacer is like a cheerleader who is swimming right

Swimming at night, under the watchful eye of the kayaker. Curtis Photography.

beside you, helping you to set a good pace and keeping you from losing your spirit. After all, like the great marathon swimmer Vicki Keith said, "A marathon swim is 100 per cent physical and 100 per cent mental."

Solo Swim Ontario also says that no pacers can be in the water with the swimmer when it is dark out. The two swimmers could bump into each other, and then the marathoner could be disqualified. Plus, it was dangerous. It was hard enough for the spotters in the kayak and the boats to keep track of one swimmer at night. A second swimmer made their task twice as hard.

In the morning I knew that one of the three pacers in the boat would jump into the water and swim alongside me. But that could not happen until the sun came up.

I still had to get through the hours of darkness.

"The boats will move away from you in the dark," my coach had told me. "It's too dangerous to have them close. But you will still be able to see the lights of the boats, and people will be able to see you."

I tried not to think about the hours ahead and kept focused on the moment, on each stroke and on each kick.

The lights on the boat could not be very bright because bright lights attract eels, and I did not want to have to deal with eels!

Lamprey eels

Lamprey eels are long, thin, snake-like fish with sharp teeth. They attach to other fish and suck their blood. Lampreys are not natural in the Great Lakes. They originally came from the North Atlantic, the Mediterranean Sea and the Baltic Sea. Although they started out in salt water, they have learned to adapt to fresh water.

Marilyn had eels bothering her all night. They tried to bite her and attach themselves to her. She had to grab hold of them and throw them away from her.

Eels are like blood-sucking snakes, with teeth that grab hold of an animal and just hang there, sucking their blood.

I could deal with eels if I had to, I told myself. But I really hoped I wouldn't have to.

The waves kept getting bigger.

There were times when I could not see

Swimming through the night. Curtis Photography.

the boat lights. It was like I was all alone in that big lake.

"We've got some seasick people," I heard someone say. "Good thing we brought the seasickness pills."

"We'll have to call the Chuck Wagon the Upchuck Wagon!" someone replied, which I thought was pretty funny. The Chuck Wagon was the boat my Aunt

Lisa was on. The boat where she prepared food for the crew.

I kept putting my face in the water and moving my arms.

I could not allow myself to get scared. If I did, I would never make it through the night.

I had to distract myself so that my mind was somewhere else while I kept pushing through the waves.

I decided to think about my friend Eric Thomas. His dad, Alistair, was the man who volunteered to organize the Toronto side of my swim. I wondered what it must have been like for Eric to learn he had cancer.

Eric was only nine years old when he stood in the doctor's office with his mother and little brother. His dad was at work. Eric had been feeling tired for a while and had been battling a stubborn fever for a few days. He just did not have any energy. He had gone for blood tests and was at the doctor's office to get the results.

He was worried about maybe having to get a needle.

The doctor came in and said, "Eric has leukemia." He told Eric's mom to go home and pack a suitcase. Eric would be going to the hospital.

Eric went into the hospital that very night. He was there for three months.

One of the first things that happened to him there is that a hospital volunteer gave him a Bravery Bead. He got one Bravery Bead for each medical procedure he had to undergo.

For three years, he was in and out of the hospital. He had three and a half years of watching his parents worry. He had three and a half years of mouth sores and nausea from the chemotherapy, and three and a half years of scary medical procedures. By the time it was all over, he had three long strands of Bravery Beads. Each bead represented something that caused him fear or pain. Each bead stood for a moment of courage.

What his parents did for him was kind of like what my parents did for me as I prepared for this swim. My mother babysat one of my pacer's kids while the pacer and I were training together in the water. My mom and dad and brother and sisters had to arrange their schedules around my training. They worked and worked to make sure the things I needed were in place, and they still did all the ordinary things that parents do, like earning money, keeping the house running and going with us to church.

They are watching me now, I thought.

Mom and Dad were at the Westin Harbour Castle hotel in Toronto. The GPS on one of the boats had been hooked up to transmit to a screen monitor at their

Chemotherapy

Chemotherapy is the term for the treatment of cancer by chemicals that kill cancer cells. As well as killing cancer cells, however, the medicine also kills healthy cells. People getting chemo have to be careful not to catch cold or flu, since their bodies may become too weak to fight off infections. Side effects of chemotherapy include hair loss, loss of appetite, nausea, bruising and exhaustion.

hotel. They could not see me exactly, but they could see the dot that represented me as we all moved across the lake.

The waves kept getting higher. They were hard to swim through. They would rise up and smash me in the face. I kept losing sight of the lights on the boats as I rose and dipped with the waves.

As the night and the waves went on, I began to feel really, really alone. And very scared.

And then I heard a scream. It was my Aunt Lisa.

Sailboats! Coming from behind us at full sail, zooming right toward our little formation!

The Zodiacs moved in closer to me, in case the intruding sailboats could not be turned away.

I could hear everyone on all the boats screaming and shouting, "Go away! Go away!" Someone turned on the big torch light and waved it around.

What were they doing there? One of the reasons there were so many rules and so much planning was to avoid just this. A marine notice had gone out to every ship. The sailboats either didn't get the warning, or they forgot, or maybe they thought it would be fun to sail right through us.

Everyone was yelling and flashing their lights. At the last minute, most of the sailboats veered away. One was not so fast, and came within metres of the Zodiac closest to me.

Boats look bigger from the water than they do when you're looking at them from the land. I treaded water and watched them speed by. They looked like giant ghost ships in a late-night movie.

The last of the sailboats passed. I heard a chorus of "Is Annaleise okay? Is everybody okay?" Then everyone settled down and it was quiet again.

I kept swimming.

And the waves kept getting bigger.

7  Endless Night

My Aunt Lisa told me later that the waves got so big that night, she was thrown right out of her deck chair — twice!

"So many of the crew were seasick," she said. "But although my boat was called the Upchuck Wagon, I am proud to say that no one on my boat threw up!"

There was no moon in the sky. At least we were going in the right direction!

I used my mind to take me out of the waves, which came at me over and over.

Strait of Magellan

The Strait of Magellan is only a few miles across but is considered one of the most dangerous open water swims. It has very strong currents and tides, and the water is cold. The first person to swim across it was American Lynne Cox.

It had been quite a year leading up to this swim. As well as all the lead-up to the swim, and being in my last year of school at Walsh Public School, where I had gone most my life, I was chosen to be a Legislative Page.

I kept moving my arms and kicking my legs, but my mind went back to being a page.

Legislative pages are kids in grade seven or eight from all over Ontario who go to Toronto to run messages for the members of the provincial parliament. You have to apply, and it is a real honour to be chosen.

In my Legislative Page uniform. Legislative Assembly of Ontario.

Pages have their own lounge and schoolroom in the basement of the legislature. We would go there when we were not on duty. Being on duty was so much fun! I loved walking in formation, keeping our corners sharp and neat, through the halls of the legislature and into the chambers where all the decisions are made. Sometimes we would sit at the feet of the Speaker, keeping our eyes on the legislators so we could see if someone needed one of us to take papers from one desk to another or fetch a glass of water.

In the weeks before we were on duty, we were given a big chart of all the members with their photo and name and where they sat in the legislature. We had to memorize it so we would know how to deliver messages. I liked knowing all their names and where they were from.

We were all afraid that we would trip and spill water on someone. There are steps all over the chamber, so it would be easy to take a wrong step and go tumbling. And the proceedings are televised, so if we tripped, it would be caught on camera for all the world to see!

One day, it happened. One of the members got water spilled on him, but a page had nothing to do with it. The water got spilled on the premier of the province — by another member of the legislature! Then, the day after that, the premier spilled water on himself!

While I was in Toronto doing the page program, I was able to keep training. I stayed with my dad in a residence at the University of Toronto and swam with the Toronto Swim Club in the university pool. They were really great to let me train with them.

Thinking about my page days got me through a good bit of time that night.

Another great thing that happened to

With my mother, Debbie. Jeff Carr.

make the past year really special was that I was chosen to be the valedictorian at my grade-eight graduation.

It was a wonderful event. I practiced my speech so often, I could say most of it by heart. As I swam, I decided to see if I could still remember it.

It started with a quote by Dr. Seuss.

"You have brains in your head, you have feet in your shoes. You can steer yourself in any direction you choose. You're on your own. And you know what you know. You are the guy who'll decide where to go."

The speech ended with: "If you can imagine it, you can achieve it. If you can dream it, you can become it. There is a lot of power in us waiting to be unleashed."

Trying to remember the rest of the speech took up more of the night.

The water got suddenly colder.

"There's a big freighter out there," someone told me. "The captain radioed us. He's heard of you and is making a wide curve around us. But it still probably stirred up some cold water from below. If you're feeling it, that's what it is."

I knew that the water around Toronto was going to be colder than the rest of the lake because of the current, and when

I first started feeling the cold, I sort of hoped we were closer to Toronto than we were. After all, we'd been making good time. So when I heard that the cold was caused by a freighter, I forced myself to stop thinking about the destination. We would get there when we got there. All I had to do was to keep swimming.

I sang the "Just Keep Swimming" song from *Finding Nemo* in my head. I sang church songs and recited the Bible verses I knew, and I watched the movies in my head about Camp Trillium and about touching the wall at Marilyn Bell Park. And I thought about Eric and his journey with cancer.

There must have been so many times during those three years Eric battled leukemia that he was very scared. He must have heard other children crying in the hospital because they were sad or scared or in pain. He must have wanted so badly to

Leukemia

Leukemia is cancer of the blood cells. It starts in the centre of the bone, in the soft tissue called bone marrow, which is where blood cells are made. There are red blood cells and white blood cells. The white cells fight infection. The red cells carry oxygen around the body.

When the white blood cells mutate, they form leukemia cells, which eventually crowd out the other cells.

go home and sleep in his own bed and go to school and have a regular life.

But imagine if he had given up. Imagine if he had said, "I don't want any more treatment. I don't like it here and I want to go home." Or imagine if his parents had said, "It is too hard for us to come to the hospital to visit you," and had not been there to give him their strength and encouragement. Eric might not have made it.

How horrible it must be for kids who

get sick and don't have their family behind them, or who come from a country where heath care is expensive and their parents don't have the money to pay for it.

I knew that when I finished my swim, Alistair had arranged for an ambulance to be in Marilyn Bell Park, waiting to take me to Sick Kids hospital so that I could be checked out. And if anything was wrong with me, I knew I would be taken care of.

Why am I more valuable than kids from countries without the same resources? Imagine if everyone had access to good health care — all those lives would be saved!

Hour after hour, stroke after stroke, kick after kick, wave after wave, I kept going. I knew that the sun would come up. It always had before. It would come up if I kept swimming, and it would come up if I said I was done and climbed up on a boat.

I knew I would much rather see the sun rise from the water than from a boat.

It was hard going, though. The waves kept hitting me. The wind was blowing hard and the darkness seemed endless.

I could hardly wait for the sun to come up.

8 Hope in the Morning

Finally the sky went from black to slate, from slate to grey, and I realized that I could actually see the boats.

It had been a rough night. My energy was almost gone. It seemed to take everything I had just to raise my arm out of the water. And once I had done that, it seemed impossible to do it again — but I had to.

"Come on, Annaleise, keep going. You can do this."

The voices seemed like they were coming at me from very faraway. I was so tired! If only I could close my eyes for a moment, if only I could sleep — for just a little while!

It was about this time in the morning of Marilyn Bell's swim when she was so aching and exhausted that she cried as she swam. Marilyn even dozed off while she was swimming. Her body went on automatic.

That's how people drown, I thought. I struggled to stay awake, and I struggled to keep my arms moving.

My legs were a different matter. They were cramping so badly that every kick brought more pain. I found myself wanting to do anything to avoid kicking — but of course you have to kick when you swim!

I thought it would help if one of the pacers got into the water with me. I could see the first one — Nancy Norton — sitting close by on the Zodiac.

English Channel swimmers

Hundreds of people have successfully swum across the English Channel. The first person to successfully swim across the Channel was Matthew Webb in 1875. A few years later, needing money, he died attempting to swim the Niagara River.

"Why aren't you getting into the water with me?" I wanted to ask her, but I was too tired to even try putting enough power behind the words so that they'd be heard. "Why are you just sitting there?"

Nancy was waiting for the okay from the swim master. He was the one who would declare whether or not it was light enough for a pacer to get into the water with me.

Finally he gave his permission, and Nancy joined me in the water. She tried to raise my spirits by making faces at me. I didn't have the energy to respond as I normally would.

During the night my coach kept trying to get me to eat, but I hadn't wanted to. I was worried that I would get too cold if I stopped swimming. Once that cold gets into you, it's hard to shake it off. Finally she insisted I stop to eat.

She put a chia-seed pancake into the lacrosse stick basket. I was almost too tired to eat. I took a couple of bites of the pancake, then threw the rest into the water.

It would have been better for me if I had eaten the pancake. It was full of potassium, which helps combat the buildup of lactic acid in muscles. It also puts back some of the electrolytes.

"Come on, Annaleise, keep moving. Move those arms! Let's go!"

Nancy swam with me for a while. When she got out, Scot Brockbank got in the water. I tried again to eat and was able to swallow more food.

Chris Peters was the third pacer to get in.

"Look right into my eyes, Annaleise," he said. "We'll swim this together. Match your arms to mine. You can do this."

My pace picked up a bit, but it still felt like I was at the end of my energy. Then Coach Lisa had a suggestion.

"I want you to drink this," she said, holding out a little red plastic cup with something oily-looking in it.

She put the cup into the net and held it out to me.

I got the cup and took a sip. It was gross.

"I don't want to drink this," I said.

"It's hemp oil," Coach Lisa said. "It will help with your muscles."

I took another slight sip and poured it out. "It's too horrible. I don't want to drink it."

"It will help you," Coach Lisa said. "I promise. Give it a try. Two big gulps, and then you can have a square of chocolate to cut the taste."

She poured me another little cup of oil.

I was not convinced.

"Do you trust me?" she asked.

I nodded. Of course I trusted her.

"Then get that hemp oil into you. It will help. You drink some, and I'll drink some with you. Okay?"

I still didn't want to drink it. Then I remembered a story that Eric had told me.

While he was on chemo, he had to drink this medicine to keep him from getting pneumonia. He hated the taste. Every single day, he had to drink this stuff down, because getting pneumonia would have been so dangerous for him. The chemotherapy had weakened his immune system, and pneumonia could have killed him.

If Eric could do it every day, I could do it once.

I hadn't come this far, through that horrible night, to act like a little kid not wanting to take her medicine. I gulped it down. And I kept it down. The chocolate helped.

I started swimming again.

Bit by bit, I felt my energy coming back. The cramps in my legs eased off quite a bit, to a point where the pain was more like an ache. I could manage an ache.

The wind was starting to calm down. The lake smoothed out and the sun appeared through the clouds that were at the horizon.

"It's going to be an amazing sunrise," someone said. "We should all take a moment to look at it. We might never be out in the middle of the lake like this again."

Everyone stopped what they were doing. My Aunt Lisa came up from the galley, where she'd been making some hot chocolate for me. Others stopped

Having a drink while treading water. Dr. Mark Ghesquiere.

their talking and checking things on the computer. I stopped swimming and treaded water. We all looked to the east.

It was a moment I will remember all my life — the sky, the water, the people around me, my exhaustion, and the feeling that I was truly alive and doing what I should be doing.

And then something even more wonderful happened, something I took to mean good luck for the rest of the swim.

A rainbow crowned the lake.

This rainbow held meaning in so many ways.

After the great flood in the Bible, Noah saw a rainbow. It was the promise that after the terrible storm, things were going to get better. After the long and exhausting night I'd just swum through, I believed that the rainbow was a sign that the rest of the swim would go well, and that I would make it.

The other meaning it held for me was amazing. The lake at Camp Trillium is called Rainbow Lake. So it was like the kids at Camp Trillium were sending me a message, too: "Keep on swimming, Annaleise! You'll get to the other side!"

So I kept on swimming.

A rainbow hovering over my destination —
Marilyn Bell Park in Toronto! Dr. Mark Ghesquiere.

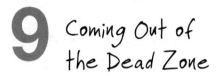

9 Coming Out of the Dead Zone

In the middle of the lake is a dead zone, a place where cell phones don't work. It's a zone of about 20 kilometres. I knew my parents were following me on the screen in the hotel, but no one was able to talk with them from the crew, and the crew wasn't able to get any messages from the shore.

We made it across the dead zone that morning, and the first messages came in.

"Annaleise!" my crew called out. "You've raised $35,000!"

My goal was $30,000, and I had passed that. Wonderful news!

A little while later, there was another message.

"Annaleise! You've raised $50,000!"

The crew was cheering. I started to swim faster. That news was just the boost I needed!

I thought back to the early days of planning for the swim.

My parents are hard-working people who, with four children, don't have a lot of extra money. Not only did I want to raise money for Camp Trillium, but I also had to raise the money to cover the costs of the lake crossing — about $15,000. Boats had to be hired, licences and permits had to be paid for. It all added up.

To raise the money I'd need to do the crossing, I had to find sponsors. This was even harder for me than swimming across the lake! I'm normally kind of shy, and at that time, I was not used to public speaking. But it had to be done, so I had to get over my fear. ScotLynn Commodities was the first to become a sponsor, and it was followed by other companies. As I swam into the day, I thought about the times I went into offices of small businesses in Simcoe to give my little speech and ask for help.

"I am asking for your sponsorship to help me swim across Lake Ontario to raise money for Camp Trillium and to become the youngest person ever to swim across the lake."

I looked around at the faces of the secretaries and clerks. They were all at their desks, going on with their ordinary workdays, and in comes this kid, whose hands are shaking as she holds the paper with her speech printed on it, telling them she was going to swim across one of the Great Lakes. They must have thought I was crazy.

There were so many of these little speeches and presentations, I gradually lost my fear of speaking in public. It became just something I had to do in order to get the bigger job done. It still makes me nervous, but it's a lot easier.

I still find it unbelievable that people gave me any money or support in the beginning. I'm very short, especially for a swimmer. Adults would look at me while I was giving my speech and they would say, "Very nice, dear," but I could tell they were thinking, *This little thing is going to take on that great big lake?* They probably didn't think I could do it until I did it. So it was incredibly kind and generous of them to support me before the crossing happened.

One of the questions I got while I was planning my swim was why I didn't just swim across Lake Erie, which is practically right in my backyard. Why did I choose Lake Ontario?

Speaking to a crowd. Curtis Photography.

Bethany Hamilton was a young surfer who lost her arm in a shark attack, yet she decided to go back into the water and become a professional surfer — with only one arm! She said, "I don't need easy, I just need possible."

Lake Erie would be a difficult swim. It is the shallowest of the Great Lakes, which means that the wind can stir it up into huge waves in almost an instant. It would be a difficult swim to plan for — water that looked smooth at the start could turn dangerously choppy without any warning.

But Lake Ontario is considered to be one of the hardest open-water swims in the world. Lake Ontario is the crown jewel of open-water swimming in the Great Lakes, in my opinion, anyway, and there is no doubt that Marilyn Bell's pioneering accomplishment so many years ago makes doing the same swim an important goal.

I also realized that what the kids and their families go through each day with childhood cancer is very difficult, so why shouldn't I try to do something difficult for them?

Like Bethany Hamilton, whom I admire immensely, I don't need easy. I need possible. And all the sponsors and help I

Lake Ontario crossings

As of August 18, 2013, Lake Ontario has been successfully crossed by swimmers 58 times. This does not mean that 58 people have done it. Some of the people who swam across it once decided to do it again.

Of the successful crossers, 3 have been older than 50, and 14 have been younger than 20.

Forty-four have been from Canada. Crossers have also come from Barbados, Italy, Egypt, Argentina, England, Mexico, Australia, England and the United States.

got made crossing Lake Ontario possible.

"Annaleise! Camp Trillium just got a $10,000 donation — from one person!"

That gave me such a boost! I wondered who this person was. Did they know someone with cancer? Did they have kids and wonder what it would be like to have one of those kids get sick? Had they been thinking about donating for a while and just needed a nudge to do it, a nudge that

I was happy to provide, if that's what it took?

It was like I got a shot of adrenaline all through me. I sped up my strokes.

"Annaleise, slow down! You don't want to burn through your energy at this point."

"I must be getting close," I called back. "How much farther?"

I can do arithmetic as well as anybody else. They expected the swim to take sixteen hours. I had started at six p.m., and the sun had been up for a while. At least fourteen hours must have passed. Surely there was not much time left in the swim!

No one answered me.

My Aunt Lisa told me later that, during the night, she slipped into the cabin of her boat to check on our position. She kept checking, yet our position on the radar screen was not moving.

In four hard hours of effort, I went only

one-tenth of a nautical mile toward my goal. Plus, I was pushed miles off course to the east and south. During that whole night of swimming, I spent most of the time being pushed in the wrong direction!

I didn't know it at the time, but I still had a long way to go.

We were getting regular reports now from people in Toronto. The donations for Camp Trillium were really starting to add up. Each time I got an update and learned that more money had been pledged, I wanted to swim faster.

I couldn't keep kids from getting cancer, but I could at least make it easier for them to go to camp and escape their cancer for a while.

The day wore on. I kept swimming.

There is a rhythm you get into during a long swim. Your mind goes off to its own places and your body just keeps moving. For much of the day I was not conscious of time

Swimming with a pacer — with a long way still to go! Dr. Mark Ghesquiere.

passing. My energy was good again, and I ate and drank regularly to keep it good. My legs hurt, but not too badly. Time slipped away with each stroke through the water.

I knew we could not be too far away.

But the sun started to set again.

I wondered if something had gone wrong.

10 Approaching the End

"We're coming up on the Humber River!"

The Humber River! That meant we were almost at the other side. I just had to keep going. It would be so horrible to be pulled out now.

Other distance swimmers have been pulled out of the water just short of their destinations. They were too seasick or their cramps were too bad or they got hypothermia.

"Annaleise! We just got another report

on the donations that have come in. Are you ready for this?"

Of course I was ready! But I didn't stop swimming in order to hear.

"The new amount is . . . $90,000!"

Wow! That was three times as much money as I had hoped to raise when this whole project began.

I certainly couldn't stop swimming now, I thought. I couldn't let all those people down.

My hands and feet were numb. The lanolin had worn off long ago and I could really feel the cold. Plus, this was the spot where it was going to get a lot colder, as the currents churned up by the Niagara River came to the surface.

I had to ignore it. If I swam faster, I would be able to warm up.

I swam faster.

I started to hear something over the sound of the water and the boats.

It was a roar.

From a crowd.

And then I saw the bright lights.

The television cameras! We were at Marilyn Bell Park!

"No, Annaleise — don't go that way!" I heard. "We need you to swim against the current. Don't keep going straight."

"But the park is straight ahead!" I called back. I kept swimming straight. I didn't know why they wanted me to turn, but I was heading for the shore.

"Annaleise! Listen to me. Not that way!"

I pretended not to hear them. I knew it was much, much later than I had planned to arrive. I had kept people waiting long enough.

"Annaleise, this way!"

And then my way was blocked. The guide boat got right in front of me. If I had kept swimming the way I wanted to,

I might have touched it, and this whole thing would have been for nothing.

I aimed where they pointed and swam the way they told me to.

Maybe it was because I was cold, maybe it was because I was tired, or maybe it was because I really wanted it to be done — but I was frustrated! I was sure the crew was making me swim away from the place I was supposed to go.

They weren't, of course. I had forgotten about the current.

We picked up the Humber River current flowing east and then it was like we were flying through the water.

The lights got really bright as we got closer and closer. The noise of the crowd got louder and louder.

I found the gap in the breakwall and swam through it, straight for the shore.

And then I was there. I touched the wall.

My journey was done.

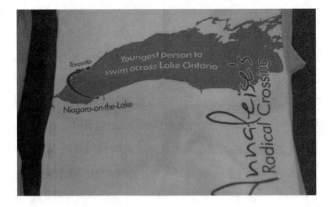

A t-shirt from the radical crossing. Dr. Mark Ghesquiere.

It took me 26 hours, 34 minutes, 11 seconds.

The crossing was supposed to be 57 kilometres, but the wind and waves had pushed me so far off course that I actually swam 77 kilometres.

I didn't care.

I had completed my Radical Crossing.

I was done.

11 On Dry Land

Real life was a thousand times better than the movies I made up.

I had asked ahead of time that Larissa be the first one to greet me when I finished. And she was! Coming out of the water, hugging Larissa and my mom and the rest of my family, getting wrapped up in a blanket, safe and sound — it was the best feeling in the world.

They led me to a chair and put me down into it. My hands and feet were numb from the cold. I wasn't crying, but it seemed that everyone around me was. They were crying and cheering and shouting my name.

It was all pretty overwhelming — the cheering, the television cameras, the reporters, my friends and family and my own emotions.

I waved to the media instead of talking to them. It was an awkward sort of a wave, but I don't think I could have talked at that point.

And I was starving!

My mom gave me one of Aunt Lisa's famous chocolate dessert squares and I just stuffed it all right in my mouth. The cameras were on me, so my mom put a towel up in front of me. She didn't want me on the television news with food all over my face!

The ambulance workers came with a

On shore at last — and so happy to see everyone! Curtis Photography.

stretcher. I got on it and we went to Sick Kids so that I could get checked out.

The guys in the ambulance were so friendly. They kept looking for my pulse, but they couldn't find it!

"I must be dead!" I joked, but then they found it, of course.

It's standard procedure for Lake Ontario

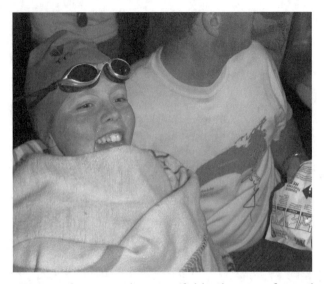

Wrapped up in layers of blankets, safe and happy on dry land. Curtis Photography.

crossers to get a checkup when they are finished. The doctors are looking for hypothermia, dehydration, anything that might need treatment. Thanks to the careful attention of the crew, I was tired but otherwise in good shape. The checkup took only twenty minutes. I was fine.

After that, I was taken to the hotel. We

stayed at the Sheraton Centre in downtown Toronto. I showered three times to get all the lanolin residue off my skin and to warm up. The hot water felt so good!

I was too excited to go to sleep right away, even though I was tired. My mom said later that I just talked and talked, sharing details of my swim with my family. They also told me how they'd felt when I was in the lake. I was so tired that I hardly remember any of that. I only remember feeling very relieved and very happy.

The next morning we had to get up and leave Toronto early in order to make it to a press conference in Port Dover. On the way home we stopped at a McDonald's for breakfast. The staff there recognized me from the news and gave us coupons for free food!

The Canadian National Exhibition gave me lots of great gifts, too — including a lifetime pass to the CNE!

At the press conference, I was finally able, along with the crew, to answer questions from the media.

It was really something, getting back home after the swim. I remembered how it felt, driving away from the house just a few days before, knowing that the next time I saw my home, I would have either completed the swim or not completed it. It was a such a satisfying feeling to have completed it.

In the days after the swim, I focused on getting ready to start high school. There was a uniform to get, notebooks to buy and all the other usual things.

Just before school started, a celebration parade was held. It moved through downtown Simcoe and ended at the fairgrounds. The grandstand was full of people!

It's always been important to me that everyone knows that this swim was not

I looked out from the stage and saw this huge crowd in the grandstand. Dr. Mark Ghesquiere.

a one-person effort but a many-person effort. My crew was on the platform with me, sharing their stories of the crossing. Diane Finley, our member of Parliament, Toby Barrett, our member of provincial parliament, and Dennis Travale, the mayor of Norfolk County, were all there, too.

Mayor Travale had a big announcement.

"We are renaming the recreation centre

On Sunday August 19, 2012,
14 year old Annaleise Carr made history.
She set a world record as the youngest
swimmer to complete the Lake Ontario crossing
from Niagara-On-The-Lake to Toronto.
Her total journey was 52 km in 27 hrs.
The previous record was set by 16
year old Marilyn Bell in 1954.
Annaleise Carr is an inspiration to all.

Members of the Norfolk County Council hold up the new sign for the local acquatic centre. Dr. Mark Ghesquiere.

pool. From now on, it will be called the Annaleise Carr Aquatic Centre!"

I wasn't prepared for that. I was speechless. In fact, I wasn't prepared for any of the activity that's happened since the swim. I thought the swim would be the end of it. Instead, a lot of opportunities have opened up, like invitations to speak to service clubs and schools. After swimming across Lake Ontario, public speaking is not so scary anymore!

It's so much fun, going to schools and meeting younger students. Sometimes they tell me that they could never do what I did. I tell them, "Of course you can! It's all about making a decision, then doing the work to get yourself ready."

My name is now carved into the rock in Queen's Royal Park at Niagara-on-the-Lake, along with all the other swimmers who have completed the Lake Ontario crossing. When I'm really old, I'll be able to take my great-grandchildren to the park and show them.

There were other honours, too, like being named Woman of the Year by the World Open Water Swimming Association, meeting Prime Minister Stephen Harper and receiving the Queen's

Jubilee Medal from him, being inducted into the Norfolk County Sports Hall of Recognition and winning the Spirit of Sport Story of the Year Award at the 2012 Canadian Sports Awards.

The biggest thrill of all, though, was knowing that Camp Trillium was getting lots of donations, many thousands more dollars than I'd dared to hope for. The donations still continue to roll in. The swim was a great way to let people know about the camp and the good work they do there.

The day after I finished the swim, I got an unexpected phone call.

"Hello?"

"Is this Annaleise?"

"Yes."

"This is Marilyn Bell. I just wanted to offer you my congratulations. You did a remarkable job and I'm so happy for you.

"You are the new Lady of the Lake."

My name is now on the rock with the others!
Jeff Carr.

MIGUEL VADILLO	40	MEXICO	
10-11 AUG 2010	18:03	SN	51 KM
REBEKAH BOSCARIOL	17	CANADA	
05-06 AUG 2011	15:33	SN	51 KM
CHRISTINE ARSENAULT	35	CANADA	
08-09 AUG 2011	22:22	SN	51 KM
ANNALEISE CARR	14	CANADA	
18-19 AUG 2012	26:41	SN	51 KM

Epilogue

What have I learned from my journey across the lake?

I have learned that our bodies have an amazing capacity for movement, and that moving around is fun! I knew that before, of course, but those twenty-seven hours of swimming really hammered it home for me. If moving around had not been fun, I never would have stuck to the training schedule that got my muscles ready to take on such a challenge.

We were created to move — so let's move! It makes us stronger, makes us happier and helps us to feel the pure joy we felt when we were little kids running around the yard for no other reason than to run.

I have learned that people like people who are passionate about something. We all have things that light us up inside — hobbies, ideas, dreams. Sometimes we get afraid to share those things. We think that other people might laugh at us. And they might! But so what? If others see you sharing your passion, the door might open for them to not be afraid to share their passions, too.

I have learned that to get something you want, you have to let people know that you want it.

It certainly isn't a new lesson. In the Bible, in the book of Matthew, chapter seven, verse seven, it says, "Seek and you will find, ask and it will be given." You might have to ask a lot of people and get a lot of no's, but if you don't keep asking, you might never find that person who will say yes.

I have learned that we do not move through life — or lakes — alone. We are supported and assisted by all sorts of people, in big ways and small.

I could not have even started my swim without the support of my family, my crew, my church, my school and all the people who donated money and time to make it possible. It was me in the water, moving my arms and legs, but I was only able to do that because others were with me — on the water and all over the country.

Just as others support us, we support others, in ways we don't even always know. When we are kind to someone, even in a small, anonymous way, who knows what sort of good effect that will have on them and on those around them? Powerful stuff!

I have learned that I am capable of doing really hard things, and of keeping going when everything in me is saying, "Just quit!" I have learned that it is possible to override the desire for comfort, to choose something more important even if it hurts like the blazes!

And I have learned that it is more joyful to give than to receive. I could not have completed the swim if I was just doing it for myself. I would probably have quit after that long night and told myself it just wasn't worth it. But knowing that the money for the swim was going to make life easier for those cool kids at Camp Trillium and their families, well . . . that made it feel worth it. That kept me in the water.

Before I went into the lake, Wally

My family and I at the Queen's Jubilee Medal ceremony with Rt. Honourable Stephen Harper, Prime Minister of Canada, and Hon. Diane Findlay, Member of Parliament for Haldimand-Norfolk. Jason Ransom.

Mummery, one of the Zodiac drivers, gave me a little stone. On one side of the stone was the word "hope," and on the other side was "faith." He said I should drop the stone into the water just before I started to swim. I did. I had hope that I could do some good with this crossing, and I had faith that I would be able to make it across.

With hope for a better future and with faith that we can do something to make that happen, we can all do great things.

What will the next stage in my journey bring? I hope it brings more of what I already have — family and faith, swimming and school, laughing and living.

I am grateful for it all.

Glossary

Carbs (short for carbohydrates): Food that provides quick energy, generally high in starch or sugar.

Dehydration: Not taking in enough fluid for the body to function properly.

Diagnosis: Identifying why a person feels sick.

Freighter: A large ship carrying cargo.

Lanolin: Fat that generally comes from sheep's wool.

Legislature: The place where elected members of a provincial parliament meet. The federal meeting place of elected members of parliament is called the House of Commons, in Ottawa.

Logistics: The details of how, where, what and when of an event.

Marilyn Bell Park: A small park along the north shore of Lake Ontario, by Exhibition Place in the south of Toronto.

Protein: A type of food required for muscle growth and organ function. Sources include dairy, beans and meat.

Radar: A way of keeping track of movement using radio waves, usually used by ships, by planes and by police to catch speeders.

Seasickness: Nausea brought on by the movement of the water.

Sponsors: People who support you as you work toward a goal.

Training: Exercises to get the body ready for a physical challenge.

Acknowledgements

So many people helped me and cheered me on in my journey across the lake. Huge thanks to them all.

Crew Members

John Bulsza — Swim Master, Solo Swims of Ontario
Jeff and Debbie Carr — Swim Managers
Lisa Anderson — Coach
Roddy Millea — Navigator
Dave Scott — On-Water Coordinator
Bill Martin — On-Land Coordinator
Alistair Thomas — On-Land Coordinator, Toronto side
Rob Smith — Head Kayaker
Dr. Mark Ghesquiere — Physician and Photographer
Chuck McNally and Dr. Bruce Bowyer — Crew of the Chuck Wagon
Humber College Sailing and Powerboating Centre's Crews of the *Ceilidh* and *Sunrise*
Wayne Boswell — Zodiac Driver
Wally Mummery — Zodiac Driver
Lisa de Graaf — Food Coordinator
Jeff McCurdy — Lifeguard
Amber Byrness — Lifeguard
Tyler Wilson — Kayaker

Acknowledgements

Nancy Norton, Scot Brockbank, Chris Peters — Pacers
Ross Keegan — Media Liaison
Theo and Laurie Vanderlee and their daughters Adrienne
   and Katelyn, Larissa Carr, McKenna Carr, Ayden
   Carr, Sharon Smith, Kate Martin, Curtis Martin, Don
   and Pam Bennett, Christine Thomas, Eric Thomas,
   Aiden Thomas, Bruce Simmons, and Monica Scott —
   On-Land Crew

The lake crossing could not have happened without
the partners who provided the resources that made it
possible. I am so appreciative of each one, and of all the
other people who contributed to the swim and to Camp
Trillium.

2nd Avenue Printing

Bachmann Personal
   Injury Law

The Beach House

Best Western, Little
   River Inn

Blue Star Ford

Blue West

Bridge Yacht Ltd., Port
   Dover

Budd's

Canadian National
   Exhibition

Catholic Women's
   League, Langton

CD98.9

Charles Jones

CIBC Wood Gundy

The Cider Keg

Clark's Pharmasave

Cooper Funeral Home

Deb Canada

Eisings Greenhouses

Erie Beach Hotel

Escapees Maple Leaf
   Chapter 18

First Ontario Credit
   Union, Simcoe and
   Tillsonburg

Good, Redden, Klausen

Grace Family Bible Fellowship

Hagersville and District Lions Club

Halnor Equipment

Humber College Sailing School

Jarvis Lions Club

John Race

Koncir Automotive

Langton Knights of Columbus

Langton Lions Club

Langton Women's Institute

Long Point Eco-Adventures

Long Point Lions Club

Lynndale Heights Public School

Marlin Travel, Simcoe

Martinrea

McKiee and Farrar

Millard, Rouse and Rosebrough, LLP

Millea Physiotherapy Professional Corporation

Norfolk County Fair

Norfolk Family Eye Care

Norfolk Hub

North Shore Runners and Swimmers

Northshore Tax Consulting Ltd.

Oddfellows, Beacon Lodge #20

Oddfellows, Empire Lodge #87

Oddfellows, Union #16

Peerless Cleaners

Port Dover Kia

Port Rowan Public School

Premium Force

Proctor Marine

Robert H. Lansing and Sons Ltd.

Roulston's Drug Store

Royal Bank, Port Dover

Scotiabank, Simcoe

Scotlynn Longhorn Group

Shaklee

Simcoe Canadian Tire

Simcoe Dental Clinic

Simcoe Firefighters Association

Acknowledgements

Simcoe Giant Tiger

Simcoe Lady Lions

Simcoe Real Canadian
  Superstore

Simcoe Rotary Club

St. Williams Lions
  Club

Suprun Wealth
  Management

Toronto Maple Leafs

Town of Tillsonburg

Townsend Mutual
  Insurance

TYR

United Alumni Drum
  and Bugle Corp

Vandenbussche
  Irrigation

Walsh Public School

Wellington Insurance

Willies at the Beach

Bibliography

Cox, Lynn. *Swimming to Antarctica: Tales of a Long-Distance Swimmer.* Boston: Mariner Books, 2005.

Tivy, Patrick. *Marilyn Bell: The Heart Stopping Tale of Marilyn's Record Breaking Swim.* Toronto: James Lorimer & Company, 2003.

About the Author

ANNALEISE CARR is a high school student in Norfolk County, Ontario. She is a member of the Norfolk Hammerheads Swim Team. To learn more about Annaleise, check out her website at www.annaleiselakeontariocrossing.weebly.com or follow her on Twitter @Annaleise_Carr. She will have a new website in 2014 to promote her upcoming Lake Erie crossing. This is her first book.

DEBORAH ELLIS is the author of more than twenty books for young people. She lives in Simcoe, Ontario. www.deborahellis.com.

Index